This Breastfeeding Tracker Log Book Belongs to

_____

_____

Dedication

This Breastfeeding Tracker Book is dedicated to all the breastfeeding moms out there who want to record all their feedings and document their findings in the process.

You are my inspiration for producing books and I'm honored to be a part of keeping all of your breastfeeding notes and records organized.

This journal notebook will help you record the details of your feedings.

Thoughtfully put together with these sections to record: Date, Time, Left/ Right, Breast/ Pump, Bottle, Wet/ Dry, Baby's Mood & Notes.

How to Use this Book

The purpose of this book is to keep all of your Breastfeeding notes all in one place. It will help keep you organized.

This Breastfeeding Tracker Book will allow you to accurately document every detail about your breastfeedings.

Here are examples of the prompts for you to fill in and write about your experience in this book:

1. Date - Write the date.
2. Time - Record the time.
3. Left/ Right - Log which breast the left or right.
4. Breast/ Pump - Circle whether your baby nursed or you pumped.
5. Bottle - Write whether your baby took their milk by bottle.
6. Wet/ Dry - Record whether your baby had a wet or dry diaper.
7. Baby's Mood - Log your baby's mood.
8. Notes - For writing any other important information, such as health, sleep, specific details, activities or activity, schedule, the food you ate, duration, etc.

Breastfeeding Tracker

Date __/__/__

Time	Breast		Pumping	
	Left	Right	Left	Right

Breastfeeding Tracker

Bottle	Wet/ Dry	Baby's Mood	Notes

Breastfeeding Tracker

Date __/__/__

Time	Breast		Pumping	
	Left	Right	Left	Right

Breastfeeding Tracker

Bottle	Wet/ Dry	Baby's Mood	Notes

Breastfeeding Tracker

Date __/__/__

Time	Breast		Pumping	
	Left	Right	Left	Right

Breastfeeding Tracker

Bottle	Wet/ Dry	Baby's Mood	Notes

Breastfeeding Tracker

Date __/__/__

Time	Breast		Pumping	
	Left	Right	Left	Right

Breastfeeding Tracker

Bottle	Wet/ Dry		Baby's Mood	Notes

Breastfeeding Tracker

Date __/__/__

Time	Breast		Pumping	
	Left	Right	Left	Right

Breastfeeding Tracker

Bottle	Wet/ Dry	Baby's Mood	Notes

Breastfeeding Tracker *Date __/__/__*

Time	Breast		Pumping	
	Left	Right	Left	Right

Breastfeeding Tracker

Bottle	Wet/ Dry	Baby's Mood	Notes

Breastfeeding Tracker

Date __/__/__

Time	Breast		Pumping	
	Left	Right	Left	Right

Breastfeeding Tracker

Bottle	Wet/ Dry	Baby's Mood	Notes

Breastfeeding Tracker

Date __/__/__

Time	Breast		Pumping	
	Left	Right	Left	Right

Breastfeeding Tracker

Bottle	Wet/ Dry	Baby's Mood	Notes

Breastfeeding Tracker

Date __/__/__

Time	Breast		Pumping	
	Left	Right	Left	Right

Breastfeeding Tracker

Bottle	Wet/ Dry	Baby's Mood	Notes

Breastfeeding Tracker

Date __/__/__

Time	Breast		Pumping	
	Left	Right	Left	Right

Breastfeeding Tracker

Bottle	Wet/ Dry	Baby's Mood	Notes

Breastfeeding Tracker

Date __/__/__

Time	Breast		Pumping	
	Left	Right	Left	Right

Breastfeeding Tracker

Bottle	Wet/ Dry	Baby's Mood	Notes

Breastfeeding Tracker

Date __/__/__

Time	Breast		Pumping	
	Left	Right	Left	Right

Breastfeeding Tracker

Bottle	Wet/ Dry	Baby's Mood	Notes

Breastfeeding Tracker

Date __/__/__

Time	Breast		Pumping	
	Left	Right	Left	Right

Breastfeeding Tracker

Bottle	Wet/ Dry	Baby's Mood	Notes

Breastfeeding Tracker

Date __/__/__

Time	Breast		Pumping	
	Left	Right	Left	Right

Breastfeeding Tracker

Bottle	Wet/ Dry	Baby's Mood	Notes

Breastfeeding Tracker

Date __/__/__

Time	Breast		Pumping	
	Left	Right	Left	Right

Breastfeeding Tracker

Bottle	Wet/ Dry	Baby's Mood	Notes

Breastfeeding Tracker

Date __/__/__

Time	Breast		Pumping	
	Left	Right	Left	Right

Breastfeeding Tracker

Bottle	Wet/ Dry	Baby's Mood	Notes

Breastfeeding Tracker

Date __/__/__

Time	Breast		Pumping	
	Left	Right	Left	Right

Breastfeeding Tracker

Bottle	Wet/ Dry	Baby's Mood	Notes

Breastfeeding Tracker   Date __/__/__

Time	Breast		Pumping	
	Left	Right	Left	Right

Breastfeeding Tracker

Bottle	Wet/ Dry	Baby's Mood	Notes

Breastfeeding Tracker   *Date__/__/__*

Time	Breast		Pumping	
	Left	Right	Left	Right

Breastfeeding Tracker

Bottle	Wet/ Dry	Baby's Mood	Notes

Breastfeeding Tracker

Date __/__/__

Time	Breast		Pumping	
	Left	Right	Left	Right

Breastfeeding Tracker

Bottle	Wet/ Dry	Baby's Mood	Notes

Breastfeeding Tracker

Date __/__/__

Time	Breast		Pumping	
	Left	Right	Left	Right

Breastfeeding Tracker

Bottle	Wet/ Dry	Baby's Mood	Notes

Breastfeeding Tracker

Date __/__/__

Time	Breast		Pumping	
	Left	Right	Left	Right

Breastfeeding Tracker

Bottle	Wet/ Dry	Baby's Mood	Notes

Breastfeeding Tracker

Date __/__/__

Time	Breast		Pumping	
	Left	Right	Left	Right

Breastfeeding Tracker

Bottle	Wet/ Dry	Baby's Mood	Notes

Breastfeeding Tracker

Date __/__/__

Time	Breast		Pumping	
	Left	Right	Left	Right

Breastfeeding Tracker

Bottle	Wet/ Dry	Baby's Mood	Notes

Breastfeeding Tracker   *Date__/__/__*

Time	Breast		Pumping	
	Left	Right	Left	Right

Breastfeeding Tracker

Bottle	Wet/ Dry		Baby's Mood	Notes

Breastfeeding Tracker   Date __/__/__

Time	Breast		Pumping	
	Left	Right	Left	Right

Breastfeeding Tracker

Bottle	Wet/ Dry	Baby's Mood	Notes

Breastfeeding Tracker

Date __/__/__

Time	Breast		Pumping	
	Left	Right	Left	Right

Breastfeeding Tracker

Bottle	Wet/ Dry	Baby's Mood	Notes

Breastfeeding Tracker   *Date__/__/__*

Time	Breast		Pumping	
	Left	Right	Left	Right

Breastfeeding Tracker

Bottle	Wet/ Dry	Baby's Mood	Notes

Breastfeeding Tracker

Date __/__/__

Time	Breast		Pumping	
	Left	Right	Left	Right

Breastfeeding Tracker

Bottle	Wet/ Dry	Baby's Mood	Notes

Breastfeeding Tracker Date __/__/__

Time	Breast		Pumping	
	Left	Right	Left	Right

Breastfeeding Tracker

Bottle	Wet/ Dry	Baby's Mood	Notes

Breastfeeding Tracker

Date __/__/__

Time	Breast		Pumping	
	Left	Right	Left	Right

Breastfeeding Tracker

Bottle	Wet/ Dry	Baby's Mood	Notes

Breastfeeding Tracker

Date __/__/__

Time	Breast		Pumping	
	Left	Right	Left	Right

Breastfeeding Tracker

Bottle	Wet/ Dry	Baby's Mood	Notes

Breastfeeding Tracker

Date __/__/__

Time	Breast		Pumping	
	Left	Right	Left	Right

Breastfeeding Tracker

Bottle	Wet/ Dry	Baby's Mood	Notes

Breastfeeding Tracker   *Date __/__/__*

Time	Breast		Pumping	
	Left	Right	Left	Right

Breastfeeding Tracker

Bottle	Wet/ Dry	Baby's Mood	Notes

Breastfeeding Tracker   Date __/__/__

Time	Breast		Pumping	
	Left	Right	Left	Right

Breastfeeding Tracker

Bottle	Wet/ Dry	Baby's Mood	Notes

Breastfeeding Tracker

Date __/__/__

Time	Breast		Pumping	
	Left	Right	Left	Right

Breastfeeding Tracker

Bottle	Wet/ Dry	Baby's Mood	Notes

Breastfeeding Tracker

Date __/__/__

Time	Breast		Pumping	
	Left	Right	Left	Right

Breastfeeding Tracker

Bottle	Wet/ Dry		Baby's Mood	Notes

Breastfeeding Tracker   *Date__/__/__*

Time	Breast		Pumping	
	Left	Right	Left	Right

Breastfeeding Tracker

Bottle	Wet/ Dry	Baby's Mood	Notes

Breastfeeding Tracker   *Date__/__/__*

Time	Breast		Pumping	
	Left	Right	Left	Right

Breastfeeding Tracker

Bottle	Wet/ Dry	Baby's Mood	Notes

Breastfeeding Tracker

Date __/__/__

Time	Breast		Pumping	
	Left	Right	Left	Right

Breastfeeding Tracker

Bottle	Wet/ Dry		Baby's Mood	Notes

Breastfeeding Tracker   Date __/__/__

Time	Breast		Pumping	
	Left	Right	Left	Right

Breastfeeding Tracker

Bottle	Wet/ Dry	Baby's Mood	Notes

Breastfeeding Tracker

Date __/__/__

Time	Breast		Pumping	
	Left	Right	Left	Right

Breastfeeding Tracker

Bottle	Wet/ Dry	Baby's Mood	Notes

Breastfeeding Tracker   *Date__/__/__*

Time	Breast		Pumping	
	Left	Right	Left	Right

Breastfeeding Tracker

Bottle	Wet/ Dry	Baby's Mood	Notes

Breastfeeding Tracker

Date __/__/__

Time	Breast		Pumping	
	Left	Right	Left	Right

Breastfeeding Tracker

Bottle	Wet/ Dry		Baby's Mood	Notes

Breastfeeding Tracker

Date __/__/__

Time	Breast		Pumping	
	Left	Right	Left	Right

Breastfeeding Tracker

Bottle	Wet/ Dry	Baby's Mood	Notes

Breastfeeding Tracker

Date __/__/__

Time	Breast		Pumping	
	Left	Right	Left	Right

Breastfeeding Tracker

Bottle	Wet/ Dry		Baby's Mood	Notes

Breastfeeding Tracker   *Date* __/__/__

Time	Breast		Pumping	
	Left	Right	Left	Right

Breastfeeding Tracker

Bottle	Wet/ Dry	Baby's Mood	Notes

Breastfeeding Tracker

Date __/__/__

Time	Breast		Pumping	
	Left	Right	Left	Right

Breastfeeding Tracker

Bottle	Wet/ Dry	Baby's Mood	Notes

Breastfeeding Tracker

Date __/__/__

Time	Breast		Pumping	
	Left	Right	Left	Right

Breastfeeding Tracker

Bottle	Wet/ Dry	Baby's Mood	Notes

www.ingramcontent.com/pod-product-compliance
Lightning Source LLC
Chambersburg PA
CBHW071407080526
44587CB00017B/3202